Scientists at Work

Forensic Scientists

Rose Inserra

Smart Apple Media

This edition first published in 2005 in the United States of America by Smart Apple Media.

Smart Apple Media
1980 Lookout Drive
North Mankato
Minnesota 56003

Library of Congress Cataloging-in-Publication Data

Inserra, Rose.
  Forensic scientists / by Rose Inserra.
  p. cm. — (Scientists at work)
  Includes index.
  ISBN 1-58340-545-3 (alk. paper)
  1. Criminal investigation—Juvenile literature. 2. Forensic scientists—Juvenile literature.
  ([1. Criminal investigation. 2. Forensic sciences. 3. Vocational guidance.] I. Title.
  II. Scientists at work (Smart Apple Media)

  HV8073.8I57 2004
  363.25—dc22   2003070428

First Edition
9 8 7 6 5 4 3 2 1

First published in 2004 by
MACMILLAN EDUCATION AUSTRALIA PTY LTD
627 Chapel Street, South Yarra, Australia, 3141

Associated companies and representatives throughout the world.

Edited by Sally Woollett
Text and cover design by The Modern Art Production Group
Page layout by Raul Diche
Illustrations by Alan Laver, Shelly Communications Pty Ltd
Photo research by Jesmondene Senbergs
Printed in China

Acknowledgements
The author and the publisher are grateful to the following for permission to reproduce copyright material:

Cover photograph: Forensic scientist Rachel Noble, courtesy of Rachel Noble.

AAP Image Police handout, p. 15 (top right); Associated Press AP, p. 18; K. Atkinson/Auscape, p. 21 (bottom right); V. Steger & Peter Arnold/Auscape, p. 15 (top left); S. Wilby & C. Clantar/Auscape, p. 6; Australian Picture Library/Corbis, pp. 16, 17; Corbis, pp. 5, 7, 11, 13, 19, 20, 23, 24; Getty Images, pp. 10, 14 (left); Jiri Lochman/Lochman Transparencies, p. 21 (top right, bottom left); Photodisc, p. 14 (right); Sarah Saunders, p. 26; Reuters, p. 23; Mauro Fermariello/Science Photo Library, p. 12; Ronald L. Singer, M.S., p. 22; © The Picture Source/Terry Oakley, pp. 4, 8, 15 (bottom left); © The Picture Source/Victoria Police, p. 9 (all); Ian Dadour, University of Western Australia, p. 21 (top left); www.brainfingerprinting.com, p. 27.

Author acknowledgements
Many thanks to Ronald L. Singer, Tarrant County Medical Examiner's Office, for kindly agreeing to be interviewed for this book.

While every care has been taken to trace and acknowledge copyright, the publisher tenders their apologies for any accidental infringement where copyright has proved untraceable. Where the attempt has been unsuccessful, the publisher welcomes information that would redress the situation.

Please note
At the time of printing, the Internet addresses appearing in this book were correct. Owing to the dynamic nature of the Internet, however, we cannot guarantee that all these addresses will remain correct.

Contents

Glossary words
When you see a word printed in **bold**, you can look up its meaning in the glossary on page 31.

What is a forensic scientist?

Forensic scientists study samples that are used to solve crimes in a court of law. They assist the police and courts of law to solve crimes.

Forensic scientists can specialize in field sciences, medical sciences, or laboratory sciences. Field sciences are used during crime scene investigations. People trained in the medical sciences use their knowledge of the human body to help solve crimes. In the laboratory, forensic chemists, biologists, **toxicologists**, and **ballistics** experts provide information from samples such as blood, drugs, and bullets.

Forensic entomologists are experts in insects and their life cycles, particularly those of flies. If a body has been out in the open and flies have laid eggs there, entomologists can use this to tell the time of the person's death.

During a crime scene investigation, equipment such as evidence bags is used to obtain samples from the crime scene. Laboratory scientists use equipment such as microscopes to analyze the samples in more detail. Computer laboratory scientists use computers for fingerprint matching, imaging (face identification), and linking with other computers.

Scientists
working together

Forensic scientists often work with other scientists such as chemists and biologists. Chemists and biologists work in the laboratory to identify tiny amounts of substances such as **fibers**, hair, powders, oils, and gas found at the scene of a crime.

This forensic scientist is making a cast of a footprint at the scene of a crime.

The role of forensic scientists

Forensic scientists play an important role in our community. Without their special scientific skills, crimes and accidents could not be solved or explained. They work closely with the police and courts of law, so that we can feel safe and protected.

Forensic anthropologists help us to learn how humans have developed by obtaining information from very old remains. Forensic anatomists use modeling to **reconstruct** faces that cannot be recognized. Dentists can also help to identify bodies by comparing the dental work done on their teeth and jaws with dental records.

Forensic scientists are often asked to be **expert witnesses** in court and present their evidence. Medical scientists and forensic pathologists examine bodies and work out how a person has died by performing an **autopsy** or post-mortem. They can then present their findings in court. The court will decide if the person who is accused of a crime is guilty or innocent, depending on the evidence. Laboratory results are also often presented in court.

Forensic anthropologists sometimes use computer imaging to identify victims of crime.

Forensic science in the past

As far back as **prehistoric** times, humans have been able to identify each other by their physical characteristics.

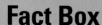

This artwork on rock is evidence of the presence of people in prehistoric times.

Fact Box
The study of fingerprints is called dactylography.

Studying and testing

Anton van Leeuwenhoek (1632–1723), a Dutch scientist, built the first working microscope in 1670. A microscope magnifies the sample so that more detail can be seen. Microscopes today are much more powerful, but they work in the same way as earlier types. Samples of hair, fibers, and other materials taken from the scene of a crime can be studied under a microscope.

Arsenic was a popular poison in the 1800s because it was easy to buy. People used it for poisoning rats and sometimes other people. In 1813, Mathieu Orfila (1787–1853) developed a chemical test to find arsenic in the body. Until then, victims of suspicious deaths could not be tested for poisoning.

Key events in forensic science	1813 Mathieu Orfila publishes the first scientific study on how to detect poisons. He develops a chemical test to find arsenic in the body.	1892 Francis Galton identifies fingerprints as a way of solving crime.	1901 Karl Landsteiner identifies types of human blood groups.
	1670 Anton van Leeuwenhoek builds the first working microscope.	1879 Alphonse Bertillon creates a system of identifying suspects, which included taking photographs of them.	1896 Edward Henry develops the classification fingerprint system further. He matches fingerprints to identify people.

Progress in forensic science

As forensic science developed, people began to think of ways to identify and record the physical characteristics of criminals.

Body measurements

How do you recognize a criminal? Italian **criminologist** Cesare Lombroso (1836–1909) studied thousands of criminals. He believed that the way a person looked connected them to a particular type of crime. For example, he believed that **assassins** had extra large heads, and pickpockets had long hands and black hair. He thought **arsonists** were likely to have long feet and hands but were underweight. To prove his ideas, he built some measuring instruments to measure the size and shape of the head, as well as developing eye tests and making other body measurements.

Photographs

Although Lombroso's ideas were not accurate, they helped other scientists to come up with new methods of identifying criminals. Alphonse Bertillon (1853–1914) created a system that meant people (particularly criminals) could be identified. His system included photographing people looking straight at the camera and then on each side of the head (in profile). This is the system now used for taking photographs of suspected criminals.

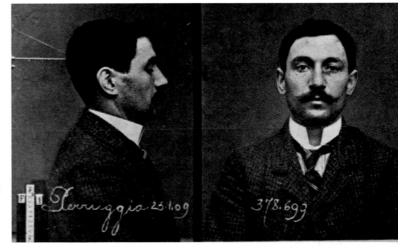

Early "mug shots" of suspects are similar to modern photographs of suspects.

1910
Edmond Locard sets up a forensic laboratory in France. He discovers that any trace left behind at a crime scene can be tested.

1925
John Larson and Leonard Keeler design the portable polygraph (lie detector).

1971
Jacques Penry develops the Penry Facial Identification Technique, known as Photofit.

1920s
Calvin Goddard develops a special comparison microscope for studying bullets.

1953
James Watson and Francis Crick discover the chemical structure of DNA.

1984
Alec Jeffreys discovers DNA profiling.

Important discoveries

Many important discoveries have helped forensic scientists find answers to unsolved crimes or accidents.

Leaving evidence behind

Edmond Locard (1877–1966) was the first person to say that "something is always taken and something is always left" at the scene of a crime. He meant that when a person comes into contact with anything, they always leave some material behind. This can include fibers from clothes, hair, fingerprints, **saliva**, skin under the nails, blood, footprints, tire prints, or tool marks. This material is known as a contact trace or trace evidence.

Fingerprints are evidence

Scientist Francis Galton (1822–1911) was the first person to realize that fingerprints could be used to solve crimes. However, Locard improved on what was known about fingerprints. He looked at the tiny ridges and the pores on them. He developed a system of comparing a print from a crime scene with the print of a suspect. There had to be a certain minimum number of similarities between the two prints before a definite match could be made.

Fingerprints can be found anywhere at the scene of a crime. Brushing for fingerprints requires special skill.

8

Fingerprints are unique

Sir Edward Henry (1850–1931) started up the fingerprint bureau at Scotland Yard in England. In the 1890s he worked in Bengal, India, for the police. He identified four types of fingerprints. They are an arch, a loop, a whorl, and a composite (a combination of the other three types). Everyone in the world has one of the four types, but their exact fingerprint is different to everyone else's. In 1896, Henry ordered that criminal record forms should not only display a prisoner's measurements but also a copy of the prisoner's fingerprint. His system of classifying fingerprints, known as the Henry system, is still used today.

Different blood types

Karl Landsteiner (1868–1943) was a medical researcher who made many important discoveries. The most well known was the discovery that there are four different types of human blood. The blood groups are named A, B, AB, and O. Landsteiner's research meant that investigators could compare the blood group of blood left at a crime scene with the blood group of a suspect.

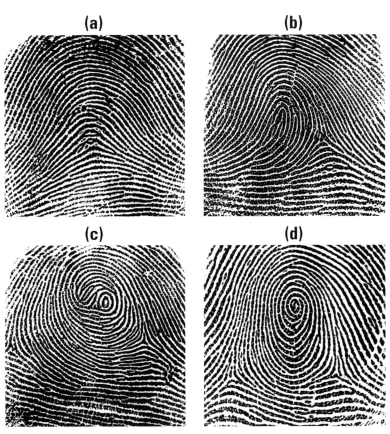

The four types of fingerprints are (a) arch, (b) loop, (c) composite, and (d) whorl.

DNA

In 1984, Alec Jeffreys and his research team developed a method called DNA profiling. DNA stands for **d**eoxyribo**n**ucleic **a**cid. The cells in all people contain DNA, and this DNA is different for every person. Jeffreys' discovery meant that samples of hair, saliva, or skin could be used to narrow down a list of suspects, or to identify a victim.

Tutankhamen: a murder case?

Dear Dr. Dig

I am doing a school assignment about Tutankhamen. I have done some research but there are many different theories about how he died. My friend Natalie said that you could help because you work in forensic medicine. Was Tutankhamen murdered or did he die a natural death?

Thank you

Abdul

Dear Abdul

The ancient Egyptian pharaoh, King Tutankhamen, was only 18 or 19 years old when he died. Many experts believe that the young pharaoh was murdered. Some suggest that his adviser, Ay, was the killer.

In the past the only evidence to prove that Ay was the killer was the result of a series of skull X-rays. Skull X-rays of Tutankhamen's preserved body show a small piece of shattered bone as well as thinning of the skull. This sometimes happens when there has been a knock to the head and lots of bleeding in the brain. Many people have claimed this is proof that the king was murdered by being hit on the head with a blunt object.

Regards

Dr. Dig

This is the funeral mask worn by Tutankhamen in his sarcophagus (coffin).

Dear Dr. Dig

What else could have caused the head injury? Could Tutankhamen have died by accident?

Regards

Abdul

Dear Abdul

The head injury could have been caused by the tools used to remove the body from the coffin. When archaeologists removed it from the coffin, its arms and neck were badly damaged. The bone splinter may have happened during the original autopsy in 1925. Forensic scientists have found what may be an insect bite on the cheek of the body's face. This may have become infected and caused him to die from blood poisoning.

Regards

Dr. Dig

Some Egyptian bodies were given a special treatment so that the person could reach the afterlife in "good condition."

Dear Dr. Dig

During my research I read that in ancient Egypt doctors could treat insect bites. Why wasn't King Tutankhamen treated if the injury was an insect bite?

Regards

Abdul

Dear Abdul

The **mummy** of Tutankhamen is not in good condition. This could be because the body had started to decay when it arrived at the **embalmer.** Perhaps the bite happened far away from the palace and the body was affected by the heat and travel. The insect bite treatment may not have been available far away from the palace.

We may never know the full story of Tutankhamen's death!

Dr. Dig

Training to be a forensic scientist

Forensic scientists work in a number of different fields, but they all need to learn certain skills. Forensic scientists become qualified by studying at college.

At school

Forensic science is a science, so high school students who want to become forensic scientists need to study subjects such as biology, math, chemistry, and physics.

Subjects forensic scientists use are:

- physics to find out information about a car or airplane crash, such as the cause of the accident
- chemistry to detect and identify trace evidence left at a scene
- math to sort and study information, especially in field work where calculations are needed
- biology in methods such as DNA profiling

Forensic science students learn about the human body in anatomy classes.

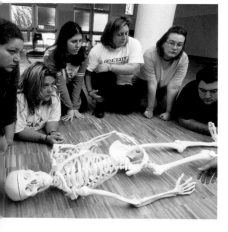

A college degree

After completing high school, people who want to study forensic science complete a Bachelor of Science degree at college. At some colleges, forensic science is part of the science degree. However, most forensic scientists have completed a science-related degree with special subjects such as biology, chemistry, and physics. Many colleges also offer a bachelor's degree in forensic science.

Farther study

Forensic science students who have completed their bachelor's degree can do more study, called graduate study. Graduate students specialize in one of the many different areas of forensic science, and do research in specific areas of forensic science. Graduate studies can take several years to complete.

After their final year of college, most students begin working as professional forensic scientists.

At work

Forensic science includes a very large number of specialist areas, such as medicine, dentistry, chemistry, explosives, and information technology (computers). Some forensic scientists specialize in field work at the scene of the crime, examining and collecting traces of evidence. Others are interested in laboratory work where samples are analyzed and bodies examined. Some forensic scientists work with computers, which may involve matching fingerprints, identifying faces, and searching for information to help police with their cases.

On-the-job training

Forensic scientists continue to gain experience throughout their careers. They continue to learn by attending seminars and conferences. They may join a scientific association, read books on their subject, and learn how to use new instruments.

Forensic scientists are always learning!

It takes a great deal of time and study to learn how to examine trace evidence.

Tools and instruments

Forensic scientists use many different tools and instruments to do their work. They use tools at the scene of the crime, in the laboratory, and in the office.

Hair in evidence bag

Evidence bags and vacuum traps

Contact traces such as hair, fibers from clothing, pet fur, pollen from plants, and paint chips are collected. This is done by pressing a special type of scotch tape to the victim's clothing, or curtains and carpets.

The traces are placed in a sealed plastic bag, labeled, and sent to the forensic laboratory to be studied under a microscope. A special container called a vacuum trap is used to make sure that the trace evidence does not come into contact with anything else.

Microscope

Microscopes

The tool most often used in the forensic laboratory is the microscope. A comparison microscope works like two microscopes in one. It is used to compare two different samples at the same time.

An electron microscope magnifies an object up to about 250,000 times. It uses a beam of tiny particles called electrons rather than visible light and can show very small objects such as soil, bacteria, or pollen grains. The stereoscopic microscope shows objects in three dimensions, rather than as a flat image.

Ultraviolet and infrared light

Stains and particles cannot always be seen by the human eye. Shining **ultraviolet light** on these materials makes them glow, or fluoresce. Washing powders, oils, paint chips, fibers, inks, and glass become fluorescent under ultraviolet light.

Using ultraviolet light

Handwriting experts use ultraviolet light and **infrared light** to look at the ink on hand-written documents. Some inks give out infrared light when they are placed under a special blue lamp. Changes to a document can be seen using the lamp.

An Identikit face

Identification systems

A witness to a crime is often asked to describe the face of a suspect.

Before computers, police used artists to sketch the description. The Identikit system was then developed where sketches of different parts of the face such as nose, mouth, and eyes were kept on file. A face could be put together like a jigsaw puzzle. Later, the Photofit system used photographs of face parts to put together a likeness of the suspect's face.

Computers are now used in a system called E-Fit. Faces can be put together quickly from computer files of face parts and displayed on the screen.

Spectrometers

Spectrometer

Spectrometers are instruments that split radiation from an object into **wavelengths**. Scientists study the wavelengths to find out about the chemical make-up of the object they are viewing. Blood samples are tested to see whether substances such as drugs, alcohol, or poison are present.

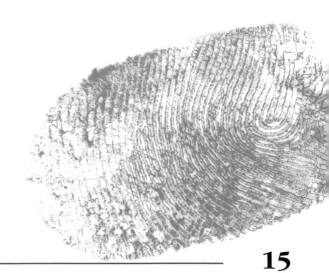

The Lindbergh kidnapping

Did the man accused of kidnapping and murdering baby Charles Lindbergh get a fair trial? Was there enough evidence to prove him guilty? Read the notes of someone who followed the case and decide for yourself.

March 1, 1932

I have decided to follow the case of baby Charles Lindbergh, who was kidnapped from his nursery near Hopewell, New Jersey, at approximately 9.00 P.M. The 20-month-old baby is the son of famous aviator, Colonel Charles Lindbergh, and Anne Morrow Lindbergh. A ransom note demanding $50,000 was found on the nursery windowsill. There was mud on the nursery floor, and footprints and a homemade ladder under the nursery window.

In the weeks that followed

More ransom notes were received, then $50,000 was handed over to a man in a Bronx cemetery. In the notes, the kidnapper assured the parents that the baby was safe and eating well.

May 12, 1932

The baby's body has been found in a shallow grave a few miles from the family home. An examination showed that the baby has been dead for about two months, probably since the night of his kidnapping. The broken skull suggested that the cause of death was a blow to the head. No autopsy was carried out and the body has been **cremated**.

Bruno Richard Hauptmann

<u>September 19, 1934</u>

A suspect, Bruno Richard Hauptmann, has been arrested. He was traced through a gasoline purchase he made using gold certificates from the ransom payment. More than $14,000 of the ransom money has been found in Hauptmann's garage.

Hauptmann claims he is innocent, and that the money belonged to a friend who'd gone to Germany and died there, so he couldn't verify his story. A sample of Hauptmann's writing has been sent to handwriting experts. They agree that his handwriting matches closely with the writing on the ransom notes.

<u>January 3, 1935</u>

The trial begins. There has been hostility from the public and the press, especially because Hauptmann is an illegal immigrant from Germany and has a criminal record there.

The strongest evidence against him has been the ladder used in the kidnapping. Arthur Koehler, a forestry expert, said that wood used for the ladder was from Hauptmann's attic, and that toolmarks on the ladder matched Hauptmann's tools.

Arthur Koehler showing evidence at the trial

<u>February 13, 1935</u>

Hauptmann has been found guilty of murder in the first degree and sentenced to death.

<u>April 3, 1936</u>

Hauptmann has been executed by electric chair.

Over the years there have been doubts about the case. Why did defense attorney Ed Reilly spend no more than 40 minutes with his client during the case? Was Hauptmann the only one involved or was he part of a criminal gang? Evidence from the trial, such as the ransom notes, the baby's sleeping suit, bone fragments, and hair samples, has been kept by the police museum and is not allowed to be DNA tested. Who knows what modern forensic methods could uncover?

Modern methods

Forensic scientists work in the field, laboratories, and offices. They use the latest technology to provide evidence that may help to solve a crime.

At the scene

Scientists who work at the scene of a crime collect samples so that other experts in laboratories and offices can do tests and give information to authorities. Crime scene investigators are called in to look for evidence. If a body is involved, then a forensic pathologist, who is an expert in medicine, may also be asked to attend. Photographs and videotapes are taken of the body and the position it was found in. Photographs are also taken of any relevant objects, tire tracks, footprints, and bite imprints.

A police tape is used to keep the public away from the scene of a crime or accident.

Samples found must be taken to the forensic laboratory carefully. Nothing must be **contaminated** or lost. Investigators wear special overalls and overshoes, and the things they collect are sealed in bags and labeled. The label describes where the item was found, the date, time, and name of the officer who collected the item.

When a car is involved, the car must be searched for dents on paintwork, pieces of broken glass, and hairs or fibers in the seats or on the floor of the car.

If footprints or tire tracks are formed in the snow, a special wax is sprayed, which hardens to make a cast. The casts of the prints are then taken to the laboratory.

18

In the laboratory

In the laboratory, samples from the crime scene are examined by different experts. If a bullet is found, a forensic scientist who specializes in ballistics can identify the type of gun used. Every gun leaves marks or grooves on the bullets it fires. Ballistic experts can match the bullet to the gun that fired it by using special microscopes.

Forensic scientists who are experts in DNA profiling are given samples from a person such as hair, nails, blood, skin, and saliva to match with a suspect. DNA is like your own personal bar code that is passed on to you from your parents. Even the smallest amount of saliva or blood allows forensic scientists to analyze the DNA.

Forensic scientists use DNA profiling to determine if two samples match. If the samples do not match, they cannot have come from the same person. If they do match, they may have come from the same person, but this is not 100 percent certain.

Fact Box

Hair can give forensic scientists a lot of information about the identity of a victim or suspect. It is very strong and so it remains on a body for a very long time. It also absorbs poison from the body.

In the office

Forensic scientists who work with computers are asked to help in cases where identification is needed, such as fingerprint matching, DNA profiling, and face images. Police store DNA profiles on computers so that samples can easily be compared to a list of people with criminal records.

DNA analysis can be done using a blood sample.

19

Working on location

Human remains and unidentified bodies are found all over the world. Who were they? How did they die? Forensic scientists work in teams to answer these questions.

The Italian Alps

In September 1991, two hikers found a man's frozen body poking out of the ice in the mountains, near the border of Austria and Italy. They had no idea that the body was 5,300 years old, the oldest frozen mummy ever found. The freezing temperatures had kept him preserved, so that the body did not look very old.

The body was taken to Austria and scientists began to identify him. The man, named the Iceman, died when he was about 40 years old. The scientists knew this because they tested the thickness of his bones. The pathologists took a tiny sample from the gut area of the mummy. They discovered that the Iceman's last meal was bread, green vegetables or herbs, and meat. On the body, the botanist found pollen from a plant that flowered in a particular season of the year. This meant that the man had died in spring.

The mummified body of the 5,000-year-old Iceman is still in excellent condition.

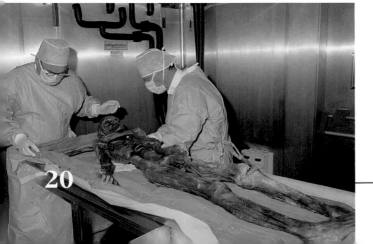

The body was taken to a special temperature-controlled museum in Bolzano, Italy. This was so that the mummy would not decay. Later, a forensic team was able to reconstruct the face with the help of computer imaging.

Insects at the crime scene

When a body has not been preserved, it decomposes. Weather conditions, temperature, and location all affect how quickly or slowly a body decays. Forensic entomologists study maggots and insects found on the body and at the scene of the crime. They can use their knowledge of the life cycles of flies to estimate how long a person has been dead.

If the body has not been buried deep underground, a fly may land on it. About 20 minutes after landing on the body, the fly can lay eggs. These eggs, called larvae, hatch into maggots after about a day. The exact length of time depends on the temperature. Hot temperatures make insect larvae grow faster, and cold temperatures slow the growth. The maggot forms a case around itself and turns into a pupa. Then an adult fly breaks out.

A forensic entomologist has to be accurate with the life cycle of the fly to give the exact time of death. A murder case may depend on a forensic entomologist to give very accurate evidence about the time and location of a death.

The life cycle of an insect can help to pinpoint a time of death.

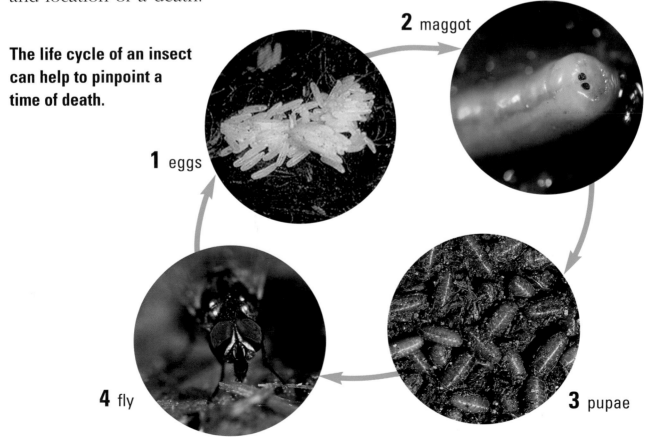

2 maggot

1 eggs

4 fly

3 pupae

Ronald L. Singer, forensic scientist

Ronald L. Singer works for the Tarrant County Medical Examiner's Office in Fort Worth, Texas. The Medical Examiner's Office determines the manner and cause of mysterious deaths.

What does your job involve?

I am the Director of the Crime Laboratory, as well as a firearm and toolmark examiner and crime scene reconstruction expert. As Crime Laboratory Director, I am responsible for the operation of the entire crime laboratory.

As a firearm and toolmark examiner, one of my responsibilities is to identify and evaluate firearms and materials fired from them. I compare fired bullets and other ammunition components recovered from bodies or from crime scenes to reference material fired from suspect firearms to determine if the evidence was fired from those firearms.

As a crime scene reconstruction expert, I study the evidence left at crime scenes to try to reconstruct the events that led up to the crime. I look at photographs, study the patterns that the blood at the scene might show, calculate the trajectories of bullets, and so on.

Do you think that television shows about forensic science are realistic?

No, most of them are not. Shows like *CSI* have to make the characters glamorous, or no one will watch them, so they combine several jobs into one, and have characters do things that cannot be done in real life.

What qualities do you need to become a forensic scientist?

Naturally, you need to be good at science, but on top of that, you need to have an inquisitive mind. If you like to solve puzzles and riddles, and stay with a puzzle for as long as it takes to find the answer, you'll probably do well in forensic science. You also need to enjoy explaining things to other people, and be good at it. You need to explain what you have done to a jury of non-scientists so they understand it well enough to use it in reaching a decision about guilt or innocence.

What do you like most about your job?

I like the fact that I am providing a service for the public. I help to expose the guilty, but I also help to free the innocent.

What are some exciting developments in forensics?

There is continuing research in DNA analysis. Soon we will be able to predict eye and hair color based on DNA left at the scene.

What advice would you give young people interested in a career in forensic science?

Get an education that is grounded in either biology or chemistry, but don't neglect the humanities. One of the most important aspects of what we do is communicate. We write reports that non-scientists have to read and understand, and we testify in front of juries made up of people of all backgrounds and levels of education.

A forensic scientist explaining evidence in court.

THE PUZZLE OF PAN AM FLIGHT 103

On December 21, 1988, Pan Am Flight 103 exploded like a fireball over the town of Lockerbie in Scotland, destroying 21 houses on impact and killing 259 people aboard the plane and 11 on the ground. The flight had taken off earlier from a London airport, headed for New York. More than four million pieces of the wreckage were traced and the airplane was reconstructed. All material that had been collected was put together like a jigsaw puzzle.

The wreckage trail sifted through by investigators included engines, control surfaces, landing gear, fuel tanks, doors, instruments, panels from inside the airplane, and the flight data recorder (black box).

The flight data recorder records everything happening in the cockpit. It showed that the control settings on the airplane were correct at the time of flight. It also showed that the engine and bodywork of the plane were normal. There had been no radio message giving a distress call.

This is part of the wreckage of Pan Am Flight 103, which exploded over Lockerbie, Scotland, in 1988.

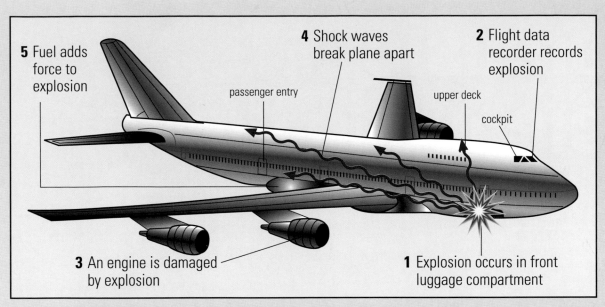

5 Fuel adds force to explosion

4 Shock waves break plane apart

2 Flight data recorder records explosion

passenger entry

upper deck

cockpit

3 An engine is damaged by explosion

1 Explosion occurs in front luggage compartment

This is how the Lockerbie disaster is thought to have happened.

A reconstruction of the wreckage showed that an explosion happened at the neck of the plane, behind the cockpit. The explosion did not blow the plane apart. It blew a hole about 10 inches (25 cm) wide. The force of the shock waves blew the plane apart. These waves rushed through the body of the plane and blew out at weak points. In three seconds the plane was in several pieces falling to the ground. With the fuel tanks almost full, the plane hit the town with the force of an earthquake measuring 1.6 on the **Richter scale**.

Other evidence about the explosion was also found:

- The flight data recorder had recorded a sound that may have been a bomb exploding.

- One of the engines had suffered damage from the blast.
- There were burn marks in the luggage compartment.
- There was explosive damage in the luggage compartment, which meant that the explosion had happened next to a luggage container floor.
- Traces of an electric device that can be used to explode bombs were found.
- Particles from a plastic explosive were found in the luggage compartment walls.

Investigators have concluded that an explosive device was planted in the luggage compartment of the plane.

Fact Box

Some action films show the hero being blown free of an explosion. In real life, someone standing this close to the explosion could be killed by the force of the shock waves.

Forensic science in the future

Forensic science has developed quickly over the past 200 years with the use of new technology and discoveries about the human body. New methods that help scientists and police to solve crimes are being developed all the time.

Computer forensics

Computer forensic scientists search for information that has been deleted or hidden on computers. They make copies of all the information on someone's computer. E-mails, Internet connections, documents, and other types of details can all be found out by these scientists. They can then use the evidence in court cases.

Computer forensic scientists can find evidence in computer data.

Computer forensics can be used in cases such as **fraud**, where computers are part of the crime. They can also be used to solve other crimes. People who create viruses that infect computer data can also be tracked down by computer forensic scientists.

One of the major problems facing computer forensic scientists is **data encryption software**. People are using coded information so that it cannot be read by other people. Only the person using the computer knows how to decode the information. Sometimes coding is used by organizations such as banks to protect personal information. In other cases, people may use coding to hide the details of their criminal activities. In the future, decoding encryption software will be an important part of solving crime.

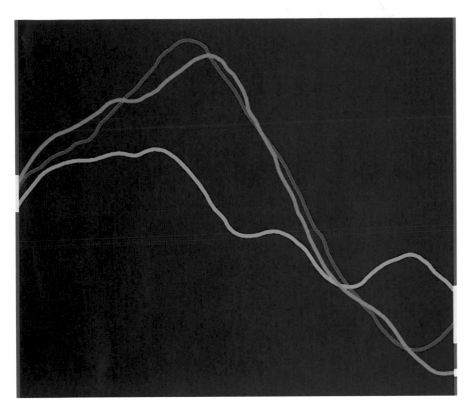
This pattern of lines represents the brainwaves of a human brain.

Brain fingerprinting

Did you know that there was such a thing as "brain fingerprinting?" Scientist Larry Farwell has developed this new system of identification.

Our brains record important events, such as committing a serious crime. Farwell uses a computer to measure how the brain acts when a person sees words that might remind them of an important memory. This method could be used on a suspect by showing them information only someone guilty of the crime would know. If their brain does not respond, it probably means that they are innocent.

DNA profiling

DNA profiling will become more accurate in the future. The equipment used by scientists will also be small enough to bring to the scene of the crime. Forensic scientists will use computers more and more to analyze the data they collect.

Get involved in forensic science

You can get involved in forensic science by creating a pretend crime scene or looking for evidence. Here are some fun activities you might like to try.

Dusting for fingerprints

You will need:
- smooth surface such as glass
- fine powder (cocoa or talcum powder)
- fine brush
- scotch tape
- plain card

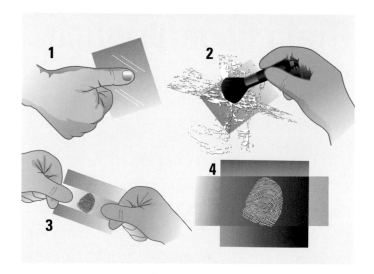

What to do:

1 Gently press your thumb onto the glass. You will see the smear of your thumb print.

2 Dust the powder over the smear and use the brush to remove any powder that does not stick.

3 Carefully press the scotch tape over the print and then peel it off.

4 Place the scotch tape onto the card. You should see a good copy of your fingerprint.

5 Collect and label prints from your friends and family.

Set up a crime scene

Someone has killed Humpty Dumpty! From the evidence you found, he was pushed from the kitchen counter. You need to decide who the murderer is (a family member or pet) and leave clues so that your friends will be able to solve the crime.

You will need:

- broken bits of Humpty (eggshell)
- material evidence left by the "murderer," such as:
  - muddy shoe or paw prints
  - fingerprints
  - washable item with some of Humpty's blood (egg yolk) on it
  - fiber samples (dog or human hairs, cotton from the murderer's clothes)

What to do:

1 Set up the crime scene by arranging the broken bits of eggshell on the kitchen floor.
2 Place the other evidence nearby for your friends to find. If the murderer is a person, you could lift their fingerprints from a surface using the "Dusting for fingerprints" experiment and place them at the crime scene.
3 Invite your friends to solve the crime.

More to do

Get your whole class involved in forensic science!

- Take a trip to a police or medical museum.

- Ask a forensic scientist to give a talk to your class.

- Take an imprint of everyone's fingerprints and label them with their names. Hang the imprints around your classroom and compare fingerprints.

Check it out!

Forensic science is an exciting science. You can learn more about forensic science, and the jobs of forensic scientists, by checking out some of these places and Web sites.

Museums

Museums as well as many police stations and fire stations keep a forensics collection on display. They may contain samples of weapons, chemicals, or burned or scorched objects used in a case.

Forensic science online

Check the Internet for interactive crime sites for kids. These sites will provide the information that you need to solve the crime.

Web sites

Ötzi the Iceman
http://www.bbc.co.uk/science/horizon/2001/iceman.shtml

Federal Bureau of Investigation (FBI)
http://www.fbi.gov/kids/k5th/kidsk5th.htm

General information on forensic science
http://home.earthlink.net/~thekeither/Forensic/forsone.htm

Information on famous cases
http://www.fbi.gov/libref/historic/famcases/famcases.htm

Glossary

arsonists   people who set fire to a house or property on purpose

assassins   murderers who kill well-known people

autopsy   examination of a body after death to determine the cause (also called a post-mortem)

ballistics   science of firearms (guns)

contaminated   made impure by being touched by another substance

cremated   burned a body to ashes

criminologist   a scientist who studies crime

data encryption software   a computer program that turns information into code

embalmer   a person who preserves dead bodies

expert witnesses   people who use their specialized training to give evidence in court

fibers   fine threads made from natural or non-natural materials

fraud   dishonesty in order to gain an advantage

infrared light   invisible light that has a wavelength longer than light we can see

mummy   a preserved body

prehistoric   before people developed writing

reconstruct   rebuild

Richter scale   a scale of 0 to 10 for measuring the force of an earthquake. The higher the number, the stronger the earthquake.

saliva   a clear fluid produced in the mouth (spit)

toxicologists   scientists who study poisons in the body

ultraviolet light   a high-energy light that cannot be seen by the human eye

wavelengths   energy of different lengths

Index